Birdwatching
Skylark ...
Teal ......
Grey Partrid
Kestrel .... ʃ
Hen Harrier 9
Lapwing 10
Common Sandpiper 11
Marsh Tit 12
Green Woodpecker 13
Quick ticklist 14-15
Cuckoo 16
Long-eared Owl 17
Barn Swallow 18
Ring Ouzel 19
Stonechat 20
Treecreeper 21
Corn Bunting 22
Bullfinch 23
Raven 24
Yellowhammer 25
Common Gull 26
Whinchat 27
Whitethroat 28
More birds 29
Notes & Sketches 30-31
Index 32

Birdwatching Tips

The aim of this series is to encourage you to look out for the birds around you, and record when and where you see them.

It is important to get to know how a bird moves, flies, and sings as well as identifying the shape, so the illustrations are there to show you important features to look out for, and the accompanying text tells you how the bird behaves.

Becoming familiar with common birds allows us to spot rarer sightings, so this book is to help you practise your birdcraft and enable you to become acquainted with the birds on the South Downs.

NB passage migrant is a species passing through

Alauda arvensis

Body length: *16-18cm*

Where to spot:

Pasture, fenceposts, high up in the sky

Resident

SKYLARK

Despite a rather nondescript appearance, the Skylark is one of our most accomplished singers, showing its fitness and vigour to predators, potential mates and rivals by performing its song while flying upwards with fluttering wings and dangling legs.

Streaks of black in the ochre and tawny plumage give the bird a mottled look.

A Skylark's song is a marathon of trills, whistles, chirrups and mimicry, lasting up to 15 minutes, and from a height of 100 metres or more.

Date	Notes

TEAL

Anas crecca

Body length: *34-38cm*

Where to spot:

Ponds and rivers with dense vegetation

Winter visitor

Teal are our smallest duck, and can form large flocks, flying in formation to confuse birds of prey; they are extremely agile in flight and burst up vertically when spooked. They gather on any fresh water including garden ponds and small ponds in woodland as they need vegetated areas to nest. The males have gorgeous colouring with a chestnut head, grey back and iridescent green eyeshadow; the females adopt a less showy look, as is the case with most waterfowl.

The males whistle repeatedly to each other.

Date	Notes

Perdix perdix

Body length: *28-32cm*

Where to spot:

Field margins, along hedgerows, farm copses

Resident

GREY PARTRIDGE

A beautiful native game bird, these have declined greatly in number due to changes in land use and lack of forage; they eat leaves and seeds so need a diverse habitat to find food, and plenty of hedgerows and meadows in which to shelter and breed. The male has a handsome chestnut belly patch but both sexes have striped sides, mottled grey front, and rufous head. They stay together in tight groups as they only fly reluctantly so flock for safety.

The call is a slightly squeaky, hoarse chirrup.

Date	Notes

KESTREL

Falco tinnunculus

Body length: *31-37cm*

Where to spot:

Above verges, farmland, mature trees

Resident

The hovering flight of this familiar falcon means it is one of our best-known birds of prey. The black band on the tail is often conspicuous as the bird perches on a telegraph pole or high branch to peruse the landscape for voles, lizards, insects and other invertebrates. The female is larger than the male (as is the case with most raptors) and has a striped tail with more foxy reddish-brown plumage compared to the greyer male.

The call is a high-pitched, rapid "kee-kee-kee-kee".

Date	Notes

Circus cyaneus

Body length: *45-55cm*

Where to spot:

Farmland, floodplains, rough grassland

Winter visitor

HEN HARRIER

Hen Harriers are among the most persecuted birds of prey, meaning their numbers have declined rapidly over the last century. The males are light grey with a white rump and pale underparts, the black wing tips being a feature; females are mottled brown with a white rump. They can be seen on the Downs as they move from their breeding grounds further north, with some birds wintering here.

They have a rather reedy voice, as well as sounding out a chattering contact or alarm call.

Date	Notes

LAPWING

Vanellus vanellus

Body length: *28-31cm*

Where to spot:

Arable fields, pasture, wet meadows

Resident

Lapwings are large plovers, about the size of a pigeon, with a distinctive crest and wide, rounded black wings with white tips. Their slow, flappy flight is also diagnostic as they move from field to field picking up worms and insects, often in large groups flying in formation. The males perform an impressive tumbling flight in spring, combined with shimmering breeding plumage to woo the females.

The other name for a lapwing is a peewit, so named for the flight call of "peee-wit!"; their actual song is more musical.

Date	Notes

Actitis hypoleucos

Body length: *18-20cm*

Where to spot:

Coastal areas, pebbly beaches

Passage migrant

COMMON SANDPIPER

Common Sandpipers breed in the northern uplands of Britain so are mostly seen on passage, or along rivers in spring and again in late summer, where some also stay for the winter. It is wader which is recognisable by its behaviour more than plumage, as it has a bobbing gait called 'teetering' and its flight pattern is also distinctive: alternating shallow, pulsating wingbeats with gliding on bowed wings.

They are vocal birds and have a diagnostic call: a 3-syllable reedy whistle, which can also be heard at night.

Date	Notes

MARSH TIT

Poecile palustris

Body length: *11-13cm*

Where to spot:

Broadleaf woodland, large gardens

Resident

A fearless little bird, the Marsh Tit frequents woodland rather than marshland, although it does favour natural rather than managed trees as here it can find cavities to nest in, and a diverse range of insects and seeds to eat; they will cache food and return to it when needed.

Its smart black cap and chin with brown back distinguish this tit from Blue or Great Tits, but they are very similar to a Willow Tit in appearance, although the latter are now sadly extinct on the South Downs.

The call is tit-like but more downward sweeping in tone.

Date	Notes

Picus viridis

Body length: *30-36cm*

Where to spot:

Mixed woodland, fields, lawns, grassy areas

Resident

GREEN WOODPECKER

Although this species nests in tree holes, they feed primarily on ants, meaning they spend much of their time in pasture and fields, flying up when disturbed with a strongly undulating flight.

The green feathers with the red head are a distinct and colourful combination. Like their cousins, the Lesser and Great Spotted Woodpeckers, their four toes are set with two facing forwards, two backwards unlike most birds; this allows for a good grip on trees.

They issue a shrill "kyu-kyu-kyu" when they take off.

Date	Notes

CUCKOO

Cuculus canorus

Body length: *32-36cm*

Where to spot:

Hedgerows, farmland, woodland, pasture

Summer visitor

The infamous Cuckoo has one of the most well-known calls, helpfully sounding its name each time. The males often perch at the top of a tree to mark their summer territory and attract a mate; they arrive in April from Africa thus signalling the start of spring. An arduous journey, and lack of caterpillar food here in their breeding zone means Cuckoos are in decline.

Females are a browner version of the male with a rippling, bubbling trill of a song.

Date	Notes

Asio otus

Body length: *31-37cm*

Where to spot:

Dense scrub, isolated copses, rough grassland

Resident

LONG-EARED OWL

Smaller than a Tawny Owl, the Long-eared Owl only raises its celebrated feather tufts when inquisitive or alarmed, but its beautiful orange eyes and sleek, tall posture are features to look out for when roosting. Their mottled feathers, however, are incredibly good camouflage. They are crepuscular so they can sometimes be seen flying at dawn and dusk, catching voles or birds.

They are mostly silent birds, although the youngsters call to their parents with a plaintive cry when hungry.

Date	Notes

BARN SWALLOW

Hirundo rustica

Body length: *17-21cm*

Where to spot:

Barns, crop fields, pasture, over water

Summer visitor

Barn Swallows return to the same area each year, having wintered in Africa. They gather mud and plant matter to build their nests, and then swoop repeatedly over the fields and wetlands to gather mosquitoes, ants, aphids and other flying insects for themselves and their chicks.

The males have long streamers; the females have slightly less showy tails but both have the red face and white undersides.

Swallows chattering and burbling overhead is a wonderful summer sound.

Date	Notes

Turdus torquatus

Body length: *24-27cm*

Where to spot:

Berried trees and shrubs

on passage

Passage migrant

RING OUZEL

Ring Ouzels are an adventurous cousin of our familiar garden Blackbird, arriving in spring to breed on upland slopes strewn with rocks and boulders, before leaving in autumn for warmer areas of continental Europe. The 'thrushy' upright stance indicates its family connections, while the white crescent and lack of eye-ring means it is unlikely to be confused with its lowland counterpart. They can be seen on passage as they head north in spring and again as they head back south in autumn.

A rich "chack" and a shrill trill are the commonest calls.

Date	Notes

Saxicola rubicola

Body length: *11-13cm*

Where to spot:

Heathland, scrubby areas near the coast

Resident

This Robin-sized bird often lives in windswept areas with gorse and tussocky grass where it both nests and hunts for its main food: insects.

The male has a characteristic habit of perching atop a tall stem where his smart white collar, black head and russet-gold breast show to best effect; the female has less dramatic markings.

They have a sharp "tack" of alarm (a little like stones being knocked together, hence the name) as well as a more melodious song with a slightly scratchy quality.

Date	Notes

Certhia familiaris

Body length: *12-14cm*

Where to spot:

Tall trees and mixed woodland

Resident

TREECREEPER

The Treecreeper can look remarkably like a little mouse scurrying up the trunks of trees and along the branches. One of the other tree specialists we have, the Nuthatch, can travel both up and down as well as underneath branches, but the Treecreeper is a little more cautious and just goes up before flying down to lower parts of the tree. They dig out invertebrates in cracks in the bark, and are well camouflaged with their spotty brown plumage.

Their call is a buzzy whirring whistle, and their song is a short trill sounding a little like a Blue Tit.

Date	Notes

CORN BUNTING

Emberiza calandra

Body length: *16-19cm*

Where to spot:

Arable fields, pasture,

perched on a post

Resident

We are fortunate to have this declining farmland bird along the South Downs as the lack of seeds, insects and rough grassland means it is becoming a rare sight.

These buntings have rather nondescript plumage with streaky markings above and a pale buff-cream belly. They use a post or other elevated position on which to sing for courtship, and they nest late in the year on the ground in grassy areas and field margins, so are very vulnerable.

Their call sounds like jangling keys making it one to listen out for.

Date	Notes

Pyrrhula pyrrhula

Body length: *15-17cm*

Where to spot:

Fruit trees, hedgerows,

wooded areas

Resident

BULLFINCH

A Bullfinch's white saddle is often the main identifying feature as it flies off in front of you. The male's bright pink breast is only noticeable in good light; the female's breast is a khaki brown. They share white wing bars and rump, and they are often in pairs or flocks of a few birds.

They like to nibble on buds so can be seen in fruit trees and hedgerows in spring, a glorious splash of colour in the sunlight.

Listen out for the call: it's a rather melancholy whistle.

Date	Notes

Corvus corax

Body length: *54-67cm*

Where to spot:

Cliff ledges, scarp slopes, fields

Resident

Our largest crow - and indeed passerine (perching bird). Ravens pair for life and breed on cliffs, roaming the scarp slopes and upper reaches of the Downs looking for food: often carrion, but they do take small birds and mammals as well as insects and other invertebrates.

They really are large, and have a definite wedge-shaped tail and a rounded wing profile with primary feathers splayed when soaring on a thermal.

The call is a classic "korrr-korrr" but a deeper, richer sound compared to other corvids.

Date	Notes

Emberiza citrinella

Body length: *15-17cm*

Where to spot:

Farmland, hedgerows, meadows, woodland edge

Resident

YELLOWHAMMER

A male Yellowhammer proclaiming his territory from the top of a hedge is a glorious sight, as his bright yellow chest shines out in the sun. The females have paler colouring, but both have the characteristic bunting wing markings: brown, black and ochre stripes, interspersed with dots of white.

The males will endeavour to out-sing each other from across the hedge or farmyard, with a recognisable song often quoted as "little bit of bread and **no** cheeeeese" which sounds ridiculous but is surprisingly accurate.

Date	Notes

Larus canus

Body length: *40-46cm*

Where to spot:

Farmland, along the coast, by rivers

Winter visitor

The Common Gull is not actually common, and looks like a kinder, more petite version of the much more ubiquitous Herring Gull. They have greenish-yellow rather than pink legs, and lack the red spot on the beak. Otherwise they have fairly standard gull plumage, and can be seen in large flocks in the fields over the Downs, as well as further inland as they look for food.

The call is more high-pitched than a Herring Gull, and less scolding than a Black-headed Gull, but lacks musicality.

Date	Notes

Saxicola rubetra

Body length: *12-14cm*

Where to spot:

Rough pasture, tussocky grassland, wet meadows

Passage migrant

WHINCHAT

These pretty chats are a treat to see during the spring and autumn, and are a stripy version of their Stonechat cousins although Whinchats tend to prefer arable farmland here on the Downs rather than heathland or coastal areas.

Males and females of all ages have a pale supercilium (eyebrow) although a mature male's is bright white rather than the creamy-buff of a female or juvenile.

They are unlikely to be heard as they save their voice for their breeding grounds in the upland areas of Britain.

Date	Notes

WHITETHROAT

Sylvia communis

Body length: *13-15cm*

Where to spot:

Scrubby areas, farmland hedgerows

Summer visitor

These warblers visit us from Africa, and the white throat is an obvious plumage marker to spot. They helpfully perch at the top of bramble scrub making it an easy bird to see if you take a summer walk through rough grassland. Both sexes flick their long tails as they move through the vegetation, although the male has a grey-blue head so is easy to distinguish from the female.

They are vocal birds, and the males sing a gruff, hurried ditty, with a slightly jerky manner as though they keep forgetting the words.

Date	Notes

More birds you may see:

GREY HERON

KINGFISHER

PIED WAGTAIL

STOCK DOVE

LINNET

You will find these in the other books in the series

Notes & Sketches

Notes & Sketches

Index

Barn Swallow	18
Bullfinch	23
Common Gull	26
Common Sandpiper	11
Corn Bunting	22
Cuckoo	16
Green Woodpecker	13
Grey Partridge	7
Hen Harrier	9
Kestrel	8
Lapwing	10
Long-eared Owl	17
Marsh Tit	12
Raven	24
Ring Ouzel	19
Skylark	5
Stonechat	20
Teal	6
Treecreeper	21
Whinchat	27
Whitethroat	28
Yellowhammer	25